HELPERS IN ACTION

A KIDS GUIDE TO BECOMING A SOCIAL WORKER

SARAH MICHAELS

CONTENTS

1. WHAT IS SOCIAL WORK?   5
Purpose of social work   9
Situations where social workers   13
Brief history of social work as a
profession   17

2. WHAT DO SOCIAL WORKERS DO?   23
Day-to-day tasks   27
How social workers make a difference in
their communities   32
Examples of famous social workers   36

3. SKILLS AND TRAITS OF A SOCIAL
WORKER   41
Traits needed   45
Problem Solving Activity   49

4. THE PATH TO BECOMING A SOCIAL
WORKER   55
Important subjects in school   58
Internships and volunteering   63

5. CHALLENGES SOCIAL WORKERS
FACE   67
Challenges Social Workers Face   71
How social workers handle stress   75

6. REWARDS OF BEING A SOCIAL
WORKER   81
Making a lasting difference in someone's
life   85

7. HOW KIDS CAN HELP NOW   91
   Empathy and kindness in everyday life.   95
   Fun activity: Create a "Helper's Journal"   99

8. SOCIAL WORK AROUND THE WORLD   105
   Global efforts to support vulnerable
   groups   108
   Cultural sensitivity and diversity   113

9. THE FUTURE OF SOCIAL WORK   117
10. ARE YOU READY TO BE A SOCIAL
   WORKER?   123

   Appendix   129

1
———

WHAT IS SOCIAL WORK?

Sometimes people face challenges they can't solve on their own, and that's where social workers step in. They are like professional helpers who know how to listen, solve problems, and guide people to resources that can make life a little easier. Whether it's helping families, supporting kids in schools, or working with elderly people who need care, social workers focus on making sure everyone gets a fair chance.

Think about a time when you felt stuck. Maybe you were trying to figure out a tricky math problem or had a disagreement with a friend. Did someone step in to help? Perhaps a teacher explained the math problem in a different way, or a parent helped you talk things through with your friend. Social workers do something similar, but they often deal with bigger, more complicated situations. They work with people who are having tough times and help them figure out a way forward.

One of the amazing things about social work is how many different kinds of people it helps. Some social workers focus on children, making sure they are safe and cared for. Others work in hospitals, helping patients understand their treatment or recover from illnesses. Some work in communities, finding ways to improve neighborhoods or support families. And then there are social workers who help people talk through their feelings, especially when they're sad or worried. Each kind of social worker has a different job, but they all share the same goal: helping people live better lives.

But why do people need help in the first place? Life isn't always fair. Some people have a harder time than others because of things they can't control. Maybe their family doesn't have enough money to pay for rent or groceries. Maybe they've had to move to a new country and don't speak the language. Or maybe they've gone through something really difficult, like losing someone they love. Challenges like these can make it hard to do the things most people take for granted, like going to school or having a safe home.

Social workers are trained to understand these challenges and find ways to help.

Here's an example. Imagine there's a boy named Carlos. His family just moved to a new city, and he doesn't know anyone yet. Carlos feels lonely at school and is having trouble keeping up with his homework because he's still learning English. A social worker at his school might step in to help. They could connect Carlos with a tutor, introduce him to other kids who speak the same language, and check in with his teachers to make sure he's doing okay. Over time, Carlos might start feeling more confident and happy, thanks to the social worker's support.

Or think about someone like Ms. Lee, an older woman who has trouble getting around because of her health. She needs help buying groceries and going to doctor's appointments, but she doesn't have family nearby. A social worker might visit her at home, help arrange for meals to be delivered, and even find a volunteer to drive her to her appointments. These small changes can make a huge difference in Ms. Lee's life.

Social workers don't just solve problems—they also teach people how to handle challenges on their own. For example, a social worker might help a teenager who's feeling overwhelmed learn how to manage their time better. Or they might teach a family how to budget their money so they can save up for something important, like a car or a new home. By giving people tools and skills, social workers help them feel stronger and more independent.

It's not always easy being a social worker. Sometimes, the problems people face are really tough, and solutions don't come quickly. Social workers need to be patient, kind, and creative. They have to listen carefully to what people say and figure out what they really need. Sometimes, it's not just about giving advice—it's about helping people feel heard and understood.

Even though the job can be challenging, many social workers say it's also incredibly rewarding. Imagine seeing someone smile after they've overcome something difficult or hearing someone say, "Thank you for helping me." Knowing you've made a difference in someone's life can feel amazing.

Social work is also about fairness. Social workers believe everyone deserves a chance to be happy and successful, no matter where they come from or what they've been through. They stand up for people who might not have a voice, like kids, elderly people, or those who are struggling. This is called being an advocate, and it's one of the most important parts of being a social worker. Whether they're helping one person or fighting for changes in their community, social workers are always working to make the world a better place.

Purpose of social work

At its core, the purpose of social work is helping people—whether it's one person, a family, or a whole neighborhood. Sometimes people face challenges that are just too big to handle alone. Maybe a family loses their home after a storm, or someone loses a job and doesn't know how they'll pay for groceries. That's where social workers come in. They look at the situation and figure out what kind of help is needed. Sometimes, it's as simple as connecting someone to a food pantry or a shelter. Other times, it might involve a lot of steps, like finding new housing, helping someone get a job, or even supporting them through school.

Helping individuals is often the first thing people think of when they hear about social work. Picture a teenager named Maya who's been feeling really down. She hasn't been going to school much and keeps arguing with her parents. A social worker might meet with Maya to figure out what's going on. Maybe Maya feels overwhelmed by schoolwork or is having trouble making friends. The social worker could help her come up with a plan—maybe finding a tutor, joining a club, or talking with her teachers about her struggles. The goal is to help Maya feel like things are manageable again and to give her the tools to handle future challenges.

Families often face their own unique struggles. Think about a family that's just moved to a new city. The parents are busy trying to find jobs, and the kids are adjusting to new schools. Everything feels unfamiliar, and it's easy to feel lost. A social worker might help by connecting the family to local resources, like after-school programs for the kids or job training for the parents. They could also guide the family in creating routines to make life feel more stable. Even small changes, like knowing where to go for help or having a friendly face to talk to, can make a big difference.

Sometimes, the work goes beyond helping just one person or family—it's about supporting entire communities. Imagine a neighborhood that's been struggling with flooding every time it rains. Houses are getting damaged, and people are worried about staying safe. A social worker might bring the community together to talk about what's needed. They could work with local leaders to organize clean-ups, build better drainage systems, or even push for new laws to protect the area. By helping the community solve these bigger problems, social workers make life better for everyone who lives there.

You might be wondering how social workers decide who to help. The truth is, they help anyone who needs it. It doesn't matter if someone is old or young, rich or poor, or where they come from. Social workers believe everyone deserves a chance to succeed, and they're there to make sure people get that chance. Sometimes, that means listening to someone's story and figuring out what kind of support will help the most. Other times, it means stepping in when things are unfair or unsafe, like if a child isn't being cared for properly or if an elderly person is being mistreated.

Social workers often focus on connecting people to resources. Resources are like the tools people need to fix a problem. For instance, if someone is sick and can't afford a doctor, a social worker might help them find free or low-cost healthcare. If someone needs a job but doesn't have the right skills, the social worker could suggest job training programs. These connections are like giving someone a map to follow—it helps them get where they need to go.

But social work isn't just about fixing problems; it's

also about helping people grow stronger. Think about a kid learning to ride a bike. At first, they might need training wheels or someone to hold the seat steady. But over time, they gain balance and confidence, and eventually, they can ride on their own. Social workers aim to do the same thing for individuals and families. They help them find stability and build skills so they can handle challenges on their own in the future.

What makes social work especially important is its focus on fairness. Not everyone has the same opportunities in life, and some people face more obstacles than others. Social workers work hard to make sure no one is left behind. They might advocate for better schools in low-income neighborhoods, fight for the rights of people with disabilities, or help refugees who are adjusting to life in a new country. Their work isn't just about solving today's problems; it's about creating a world where everyone has a fair shot at success.

Sometimes, social workers help people through really tough situations, like natural disasters or emergencies. Imagine what it's like after a hurricane destroys homes in a town. Families might be separated, and people might not know where to go for help. Social workers step in to provide support, whether it's finding shelter, reuniting families, or just offering someone a shoulder to lean on. In these moments, social workers are like the glue holding everything together, helping people get back on their feet.

Helping a community doesn't always mean fixing something that's broken. Sometimes, it's about making good things happen. A social worker might work with kids in a neighborhood to start a sports league or an art program. These activities bring people together, create friendships, and give kids a positive way to spend their time. By focusing on building strong communities, social workers help prevent problems before they start.

Situations where social workers

Social workers encounter all kinds of situations every day. Their job is to meet people where they are and help them navigate challenges that might seem impossible to solve. Sometimes, it's about helping children who need a safe place to live. Other times, it's about supporting families who are struggling to get by or assisting someone with a disability who wants to live independently. Let's look at some examples of what social workers do and how their work can change lives.

Take a moment to think about a child who doesn't

have a safe home. Maybe their parents are unable to take care of them because of serious problems, like illness or addiction. Without someone to step in, that child might not have food to eat, a warm bed, or even someone to hug them when they feel scared. A social worker's job is to help. They work to find a foster family—people who can provide a loving and secure home until things get better. They don't just stop there, though. Social workers keep checking in, making sure the child is happy and safe. If possible, they help reunite the child with their parents when the situation improves.

Now think about a family that's going through hard times. Maybe one parent lost their job, and the bills are piling up. The family might worry about losing their home or not having enough to eat. A social worker can be like a guide, helping them figure out what to do next. They might connect the family with food banks or programs that help pay rent. Sometimes, they'll sit down with the parents to create a budget, teaching them how to make their money stretch farther. It's not just about solving the immediate problem—it's about giving the family tools to stay on their feet in the future.

Then there are people with disabilities, who might need extra help to live independently. Imagine someone who uses a wheelchair but lives in a house with stairs. That could make even simple things, like getting to the front door, feel like an obstacle course. A social worker could help them find resources to make their home more accessible, like ramps or stair lifts. They might also connect them with job training programs or support groups where they can meet others facing similar challenges. The goal is to help them live life to the fullest, in a way that works for them.

Social workers often help during emergencies, too. Picture a community hit by a hurricane. Homes are flooded, schools are closed, and families are separated. It's chaos. Social workers jump into action, helping people find temporary housing, access food and water, and reunite with loved ones. They might also provide emotional support, listening to people's stories and helping them cope with what they've been through. Even after the immediate crisis is over, social workers stick around, helping the community rebuild and prepare for the future.

Sometimes, social workers focus on helping kids in schools. Imagine a boy named Liam, who's always getting into trouble. His teachers think he's just being difficult, but a social worker might take the time to figure out what's really going on. Maybe Liam is acting out because he's struggling with reading and feels embarrassed. Or maybe there's a problem at home that's making it hard for him to concentrate. The social worker could work with Liam's teachers to create a plan, like giving him extra help with reading or setting up a quiet space where he can focus. By understanding what Liam needs, they can help him succeed.

Another important part of a social worker's job is helping people who feel alone or overwhelmed. Think about an elderly woman named Mrs. Thompson, who lives by herself. Her husband passed away, and her kids live far away. She feels lonely and has trouble doing everyday things like grocery shopping. A social worker might visit her and find ways to make her life easier, like arranging for meals to be delivered or connecting her with a local senior center where she can make new friends. Sometimes, just having someone to talk to can make a huge difference.

There are also times when social workers step in to help people who feel like they've lost their way. Imagine a teenager named Jordan, who's been skipping school and hanging out with the wrong crowd. Jordan feels like no one understands him, and he's not sure what to do with his life. A social worker might sit down with Jordan and really listen, without judgment.

They could help him figure out his goals and find programs that match his interests, like sports teams or job training courses. By showing Jordan that someone believes in him, the social worker can help him see a brighter future.

In every one of these situations, social workers are doing more than just solving problems. They're building connections and creating hope. It's not always about having all the answers—it's about helping people find the answers that work best for them. Sometimes, that means connecting them to resources. Other times, it means being a shoulder to lean on or a voice of encouragement.

Brief history of social work as a profession

A long time ago, in many parts of the world, families and neighbors looked after each other. If someone couldn't work because they were sick or too old, others would pitch in to help. This kind of care was often based on kindness and shared responsibility. In medieval Europe, for example, churches played a big role in helping people. Monks and nuns would run hospitals for the sick, orphanages for children, and shelters for travelers who had nowhere else to stay.

But as towns and cities grew bigger, life got more

complicated. By the 1600s, in places like England, there were so many people in need that communities couldn't handle everything on their own. This led to the creation of something called the Poor Laws. These were rules that said local governments had to take care of poor people, but the help wasn't always kind or fair. Some people were sent to workhouses, places where they had to work very hard in exchange for food and shelter. These workhouses were often harsh and uncomfortable, and people avoided them if they could.

Fast forward to the 1800s, when the Industrial Revolution changed everything. Factories and machines made it easier to produce goods, but they also created problems. Many people moved to cities to find work, but not everyone succeeded. Families lived in crowded, dirty conditions, and some didn't have enough food or clean water. This was a time when social work started to take shape. People began to realize that charity wasn't enough—there needed to be better ways to solve problems.

One of the first big steps toward modern social work happened in England with something called the Charity Organization Society, or COS for short. The COS believed in helping people, but they wanted to do it in a way that made a lasting difference. Instead of just giving money or food, they tried to figure out why people were struggling and what could be done to fix the root causes. They trained people, known as "friendly visitors," to meet with families and help them make plans to improve their lives. These visitors were the early version of social workers.

Around the same time, something exciting was happening in the United States. A woman named Jane Addams opened a place called Hull House in Chicago in 1889. Hull House wasn't just a shelter—it was a community center where people could take classes, learn new skills, and get help with problems like finding a job or caring for their children. Jane Addams and the other workers at Hull House believed that everyone, no matter how poor, deserved respect and opportunities to succeed. Hull House became famous, and other cities started opening similar centers.

This period also saw the rise of something called settlement houses. These were places where social workers lived alongside the people they helped. The idea was to understand people's lives by experiencing them firsthand. This made social work different from other kinds of help. It wasn't about looking down on people or giving orders—it was about working together to create solutions.

By the early 1900s, social work was becoming more

professional. Schools started offering courses to train social workers, and organizations were created to set standards for the profession. One of the first schools of social work was at Columbia University in New York. Students learned about psychology, economics, and other subjects that could help them understand and assist people better. This was an important step because it showed that social work wasn't just about good intentions—it was a skill that could be taught and improved.

During this time, social workers began focusing on specific areas, like helping children, supporting workers, and improving housing. They worked in hospitals, schools, and government offices, always looking for ways to make life better for those who needed help. One of the key ideas was that everyone deserved dignity and fairness, no matter their background.

The Great Depression in the 1930s brought new challenges for social workers. Millions of people lost their jobs and homes, and poverty was everywhere. Social workers worked tirelessly to connect families to programs that provided food, housing, and other necessities. This was also when the government started taking a bigger role in helping people, creating programs like Social Security to support older adults and unemployed workers.

Later, during the Civil Rights Movement in the 1950s and 1960s, social workers played an important role in fighting for equality. They worked to end discrimination and ensure that everyone had access to education, healthcare, and jobs. This was a time when social workers weren't just helping individuals—they were also pushing for changes in laws and policies to make society fairer for everyone.

2

WHAT DO SOCIAL WORKERS DO?

I magine walking through a busy city. People are everywhere—kids heading to school, parents rushing to work, someone in a hospital gown being wheeled to a car, and groups chatting at a community center. You might not notice it, but social workers are often quietly working behind the scenes in places like these, helping to make life better for those who need it. Social workers don't just have one job. Depending on where they work, they focus on different kinds of problems and people. Let's step into their shoes and see what they do in schools, hospitals, communities, and family services.

Start with a school. Picture a big building buzzing with energy—kids laughing in the hallways, teachers giving lessons, and bells ringing to mark the start of each class. It seems like everything is running smoothly, but sometimes things aren't as perfect as they appear. Maybe there's a student who's having trouble keeping up with their schoolwork. Perhaps they don't have a quiet place to study at home, or they're distracted because their parents are going through a divorce. This is where a school social worker steps in. They don't teach math or history, but their work is just as important.

A school social worker's job is to make sure students can focus on learning. They meet with students who are struggling and figure out what's causing the problem. Sometimes they'll work with teachers to adjust assignments for a student who's having a tough time. Other times, they'll help connect the student's family with resources, like a counselor or after-school programs. Imagine a girl named Ava who keeps skipping class because she feels overwhelmed. A social worker might meet with her, listen to her worries, and help her build a plan to manage her stress. They're like detectives, finding the root of a problem and working with others to fix it.

Now, let's head to a hospital. Hospitals can be overwhelming places with machines beeping, doctors hurrying between patients, and families anxiously waiting for news. While doctors and nurses focus on physical health, hospital social workers care for the emotional and practical needs of patients and their families. They're there to ask questions like, "How are you holding up?" and "What can we do to make this easier for you?"

Imagine a boy named Ethan who's in the hospital for surgery. His parents are worried, not just about Ethan's recovery but also about how they'll pay the medical bills. A hospital social worker might meet with them to talk through their concerns. They could explain what insurance might cover, help them apply for financial aid, or connect them with a support group for parents of kids with similar conditions. They might also talk to Ethan, helping him understand what's happening and making sure he feels as comfortable as possible. It's not just about treating the illness—it's about making sure the whole family feels supported during a tough time.

Next, picture a bustling community center. This is where community social workers often focus their efforts. Their job is all about making neighborhoods better places to live. They might organize programs to help people learn new skills, like computer classes for adults or art workshops for kids. Sometimes, they help entire neighborhoods work together to solve problems, like fixing a playground or improving safety.

Think about a neighborhood that's been struggling with too much traffic near a school. A community social worker might gather parents, teachers, and local leaders to come up with solutions, like adding a crossing guard or speed bumps. They're not just helping one person—they're helping everyone in the area. Community social workers believe in the power of teamwork. When people come together, amazing things can happen.

Finally, let's step into a family's home. Family social workers focus on helping families stay strong and connected, even when life gets tough. Sometimes, they help parents who are struggling to care for their kids. Other times, they work with families going through big changes, like adopting a child or dealing with a loss. Their goal is to make sure families have the tools they need to support each other.

Imagine a family with two kids, Sofia and Mateo, whose parents are going through a rough patch. There's a lot of arguing, and the kids are starting to feel anxious. A family social worker might visit their home and talk with everyone to understand what's going on. They could suggest ways for the parents to communicate better or help the kids express their feelings in healthy ways. By helping the family work through their problems, the social worker is creating a more peaceful and supportive home environment.

While school, hospital, community, and family social workers focus on different things, they all have something in common: they listen. Social workers don't assume they know the answers right away. They take the time to hear people's stories and understand what they're going through. This helps them figure out the best way to help.

Social workers also know how to work with other professionals. A school social worker might team up with teachers and counselors. A hospital social worker could collaborate with doctors and nurses. A community social worker might meet with city planners or local officials. Family social workers often partner with therapists or child welfare agencies. They're like the glue that holds everyone together, making sure all the pieces fit.

Day-to-day tasks

A social worker's day is often busy, surprising, and full of challenges, but it's also filled with opportunities to make a real difference.

Let's start with one of the most important parts of a social worker's day: meeting with people. This might happen in an office, at a school, in a hospital room, or even at someone's home. Each meeting is unique because every person has their own story and their own set of problems. Some people might feel nervous or shy about sharing what's going on in their lives. Social workers know how to make people feel comfortable, starting with simple questions like, "How are you feeling today?" or "What's been going on?"

Think about a social worker meeting with a teenager named Liam. Liam has been feeling over-whelmed at school and doesn't know how to handle the pressure. The social worker listens carefully, letting Liam explain his worries without interrupting. They might ask questions to help Liam figure out what's bothering him the most. Maybe it's the fear of failing a math test, or maybe it's feeling left out by friends. By listening, the social worker starts to under-stand Liam's challenges and can begin to help him work through them.

Once a social worker understands what someone is dealing with, the next step is problem-solving. This can feel a bit like putting together a puzzle. Each piece of information—whether it's about someone's family, school, health, or job—helps the social worker figure out what might make things better. Sometimes the solutions are simple, like helping someone write a resume or find a local food bank. Other times, the problems are more complex and need creative thinking.

Take, for example, a single mom named Maria, who's worried about paying rent after losing her job. The social worker might help Maria explore her options, like applying for temporary financial assistance or looking for job training programs. They might even help Maria write job applications or practice for interviews. Maria's problem isn't solved in one meeting, but the social worker's guidance helps her take the first steps toward a solution.

Another key part of a social worker's day is connecting people to resources. This might sound like handing someone a list of phone numbers, but it's much more than that. Social workers often spend hours researching and building relationships with local organizations, charities, and government programs. They know who to call and what questions to ask to make sure people get the help they need.

Imagine a family with a young boy named Alex who has a disability. Alex's parents want him to have the best opportunities, but they don't know where to start. A social worker might help the family find resources like physical therapy, special education programs, or even a summer camp designed for kids with disabilities. They could also connect the parents with support groups where they can meet other families facing similar challenges. By finding these resources, the social worker helps Alex's family feel less alone and more prepared to handle their situation.

Sometimes, social workers are like investigators, digging deep to uncover the details of a problem. They might visit someone's home to see how they're living or check in with teachers, doctors, or neighbors to get a fuller picture of what's going on. This kind of work takes patience and determination, but it's essential for making sure the right help is provided.

For example, imagine a social worker is helping a little girl named Mia, who isn't doing well in school. The teacher says Mia seems tired all the time and often forgets her homework. The social worker visits Mia's home and finds that her family has been struggling since her dad lost his job. They've had to move in with relatives, and Mia doesn't have a quiet place to study or sleep. With this new information, the social worker can help Mia's family find a more stable living situation and support Mia at school.

Social workers also spend time on the phone or writing reports. While this might not sound as exciting as meeting with people, it's just as important.

Reports help keep track of what's been done and what still needs to happen. For example, if a social worker is helping a foster child, they might write a report about how the child is adjusting to their new home. These reports are shared with other professionals, like teachers or case managers, to make sure everyone is on the same page.

Sometimes, social workers work with groups instead of individuals. They might lead a class on parenting skills, organize a community event, or run a support group for people dealing with similar problems. These group settings can be powerful because they bring people together. Imagine a support group for teenagers who've lost a parent. At first, they might feel shy about talking, but as they hear others share their feelings, they start to realize they're not alone. The social worker helps guide the conversation, creating a safe space for everyone to share and heal.

Of course, a social worker's day isn't always predictable. Emergencies can happen, and social workers have to be ready to respond. They might get a call from a hospital about a patient who needs immediate help finding a place to stay after being discharged. Or they might hear from a school about a child who hasn't shown up for days and seems to be in trouble. These moments can be stressful, but they're also where social workers shine, using their skills to step in and make a difference.

One of the most important things social workers do each day is build trust. Many of the people they work with are dealing with tough situations and might feel nervous about accepting help. Social workers take the time to show that they care, not just through their words but through their actions. Whether it's showing up for a meeting on time, following through on a promise, or just being a calm and steady presence, these small things help build the trust that makes their work possible.

How social workers make a difference in their communities

Social workers don't just help individuals or families —they work to improve entire neighborhoods. When they see problems that affect many people, they think about solutions that can bring everyone together. Sometimes that means creating programs to meet specific needs, and other times it's about connecting groups of people to solve bigger challenges.

Take a look at a community center in a busy city. This might be where a social worker organizes programs for families, like free classes on budgeting or parenting skills. Imagine a mom named Lisa who just had a baby and feels unsure about how to balance work, caring for her child, and managing bills. She attends a class run by a social worker and learns helpful tips for organizing her time and saving money. But the class does more than that—it gives Lisa a chance to meet other moms who are going through the same things. Suddenly, she feels less alone, and she has new friends who can share advice and encouragement. That's the power of a community program led by a social worker.

Social workers also focus on helping kids feel safe and supported in their neighborhoods. Let's say there's a group of kids who don't have a park nearby to play in. They're bored after school and might end up wandering the streets, which isn't always safe. A social worker could meet with the kids, their parents, and local leaders to talk about building a park or creating after-school activities. Maybe they work together to open a youth center with games, sports, and homework help. Now the kids have a fun place to go, and the neighborhood feels like a better, safer place to live.

But what about people who don't often ask for help, like the elderly man down the street? Social workers make a difference here too. They might check in on people who live alone to see how they're doing.

Imagine this man, Mr. Rodriguez, who used to love gardening but now struggles to keep up with it because of his age. A social worker might arrange for a volunteer to help him with his garden or invite him to join a gardening group at the local senior center. Not only does Mr. Rodriguez get back to doing what he loves, but he also makes new friends and feels connected to his community again.

Sometimes, social workers help neighborhoods prepare for emergencies. Picture a small town near a river that floods every few years. The flooding damages homes and leaves families without electricity or clean water. A social worker might work with local leaders to set up an emergency plan. They could organize a community meeting to teach families what to do during a flood, like where to find shelters or how to protect their belongings. When the next flood comes, the town is ready, and fewer people are left without help.

Social workers also make a difference by standing up for people who might not have a voice. Let's say there's a school where kids with disabilities aren't getting the support they need. A social worker might work with the school's teachers and parents to make changes, like adding ramps for wheelchairs or hiring more aides to help in classrooms. These changes don't just help one or two kids—they make the school a better place for everyone.

Another way social workers improve communities is by helping people find jobs. Imagine a factory in a town closes, leaving hundreds of people without work. A social worker might organize job fairs or connect people to training programs for new skills. Take the example of James, a factory worker who hasn't written a resume in years. With the social worker's help, James learns how to highlight his skills and apply for jobs online. Soon, he finds a new job, and he feels proud of what he's accomplished.

Communities are stronger when everyone has a chance to succeed. Social workers understand this, and they often focus on creating opportunities for people who might otherwise be left out. This could mean organizing a program to help refugees adjust to life in a new country or working with city officials to improve public transportation so more people can get to work and school.

One of the most powerful things social workers do in communities is bring people together. Sometimes, when there's a big problem, it can feel overwhelming to solve it alone. Social workers act as leaders, helping people find ways to work as a team. Imagine a neighborhood with a vacant lot that's become a dumping ground for trash. Instead of waiting for someone else to fix it, a social worker might bring neighbors together to clean up the lot and turn it into a community garden. Now, instead of being an eyesore, the space becomes a beautiful place where people can grow vegetables and flowers while getting to know each other.

What makes all of this work so important is that it creates a ripple effect. When one part of a community improves, it often leads to other positive changes. For example, when kids have a safe place to play, they're more likely to stay out of trouble. When parents learn how to manage their money, they can provide a more stable home for their families. When elderly people feel connected, they're healthier and happier. And when neighbors work together, they create a stronger, more caring community.

Examples of famous social workers

One name that stands out in the history of social work is Jane Addams. She grew up in Illinois in the 1800s and always had a big heart for people in need. When she visited London as a young woman, she saw a place called Toynbee Hall, where wealthy people and those in poverty lived and worked together to learn from one another. This idea inspired Jane. When she returned to the United States, she founded Hull House in Chicago in 1889.

Hull House wasn't just a shelter. It was a place where people could take art classes, learn English, or get help finding a job. Jane believed in treating everyone with respect, no matter how poor they were. She even lived at Hull House herself, showing she was part of the community. Jane's work helped thousands of immigrants and families in Chicago, and her ideas spread to other cities. She also became the first American woman to win the Nobel Peace Prize for her work promoting peace and equality. Jane showed that kindness and determination could bring people together and create real change.

Another inspiring figure is Frances Perkins. She didn't start her career as a social worker, but her work helped shape many of the social programs we have today. Frances grew up in Massachusetts in the early 1900s and cared deeply about workers' rights. One day, she witnessed a terrible tragedy: a factory fire in New York City that killed over 100 workers, many of them young women. Frances was determined to make sure something like that never happened again.

She became the first woman to serve in a U.S. presidential cabinet, working as Secretary of Labor under

President Franklin D. Roosevelt. Frances helped create laws to protect workers, like safety rules for factories and the 40-hour workweek. She also played a key role in creating Social Security, which provides financial support for retired people and those with disabilities. Frances used her position to fight for fairness and dignity, showing how social work can lead to big changes that help millions of people.

Eglantyne Jebb is another social worker whose impact reached far beyond her own community. She was born in England and worked as a teacher before dedicating her life to helping children. During World War I, Eglantyne was heartbroken by the suffering of children caught in the middle of the fighting. She believed that every child, no matter where they lived, deserved to be safe, healthy, and educated.

In 1919, Eglantyne founded Save the Children, an organization that still exists today and helps children around the world. She also wrote the first version of what became the United Nations Convention on the Rights of the Child, a document that outlines the rights every child should have, like the right to play and the right to an education. Eglantyne's work reminds us that social workers don't just help individuals—they can change the way the world treats its most vulnerable people.

Closer to our own time, there's Dorothy Height, who dedicated her life to fighting for civil rights and social justice. Dorothy grew up in Pennsylvania and was an excellent student. She won a college scholarship but was turned away because the school didn't accept African American students. Instead of giving up, Dorothy attended another college and used her education to work for equality.

Dorothy became a leader in the Civil Rights Movement, working alongside people like Martin Luther King Jr. and Rosa Parks. She focused on issues like racial inequality, education, and women's rights. Dorothy also served as president of the National Council of Negro Women for more than 40 years. Through her leadership, she helped create programs to support families, improve schools, and empower women to achieve their goals. Dorothy's work showed that social workers can be powerful advocates for justice and equality.

Another name to know is Muhammad Yunus, who used his background in economics to make a difference for poor communities in Bangladesh. Muhammad noticed that many people in his country, especially women, struggled to start small businesses because they couldn't get loans from banks. Without these loans, they couldn't buy the materials they needed to grow crops, sew clothes, or open shops.

In response, Muhammad started something called microcredit, which provides small loans to people who don't have access to traditional banks. He founded the Grameen Bank, which has helped millions of people lift themselves out of poverty. Muhammad won the Nobel Peace Prize for his innovative approach, and his work continues to inspire social workers who focus on economic justice.

There are also countless social workers who might not be famous but have changed lives in powerful ways. For example, consider Clara Barton, who is best known for founding the American Red Cross. Clara wasn't officially a social worker, but her work helping soldiers during the Civil War and organizing disaster relief set the stage for many of the things social workers do today. She showed how compassion and quick thinking could save lives and bring communities together during difficult times.

3

SKILLS AND TRAITS OF A SOCIAL WORKER

One of the first and most important skills a social worker has is listening. You might think, "How hard can it be to listen?" But there's a big difference between hearing someone's words and truly understanding what they mean. Imagine a boy named Jason who tells a social worker, "I hate school." It might sound like he's just complaining, but a good listener would notice how Jason says it. Is he angry? Sad? Quiet? Listening carefully helps the social worker figure out what's really going on. Maybe Jason feels lonely at school, or maybe he's struggling with his homework and feels embarrassed. By paying attention, the social worker can uncover the real problem.

Listening isn't just about hearing words; it's about

noticing what people don't say, too. Let's say a mom named Maria comes to a social worker and talks about her kids. She says they're doing fine, but she avoids eye contact and fidgets with her hands. A skilled listener might wonder if Maria is worried about something she's not ready to share. Maybe she's afraid of being judged, or maybe she doesn't know how to ask for help. The social worker might gently ask a few questions, creating a safe space for Maria to open up. This kind of listening shows people that their feelings matter, even if they're hard to talk about.

Another key skill is empathy. Empathy means understanding how someone else feels, even if you haven't experienced the same thing yourself. It's like stepping into their shoes and seeing the world from their perspective. For a social worker, empathy is essential because they work with people who are often going through tough times. Imagine a teenager named Sophie who's upset because her parents are getting divorced. A social worker might not have been through a divorce themselves, but they can still imagine how scary and uncertain it must feel for Sophie. By showing empathy, the social worker lets Sophie know she's not alone and that her feelings are valid.

Empathy isn't about fixing someone's problems

right away. It's about being there for them and showing that you care. Sometimes, just saying, "That sounds really hard," or "I can see why you'd feel that way," can make a huge difference. It's like offering a hand to hold when someone feels like they're walking through a storm.

Problem-solving is another skill every social worker needs. Life can be complicated, and the people social workers help often face challenges with no easy answers. Think of it like a puzzle where some of the pieces are missing. A social worker has to figure out how to make things work anyway. For example, imagine a family that's struggling to afford groceries. The social worker might look for food banks nearby, help the parents apply for financial assistance, or even teach them how to budget their money. Problem-solving isn't about knowing all the answers right away; it's about being creative and resourceful.

Sometimes, solving problems means thinking ahead. Imagine a town that floods every spring. A social worker might work with the community to create an emergency plan before the next flood hits. They could organize a meeting where families learn what to pack in an emergency kit or where to find shelters. By planning ahead, the social worker helps people feel prepared and less afraid when the flood-waters come.

Of course, none of this would work without good communication. Social workers have to explain complicated things in ways that make sense to every-one. Imagine trying to explain how health insurance works to someone who's never had it before. It's full of confusing words like "deductible" and "premium." A social worker might break it down into simple steps, using examples to make it easier to understand. Clear communication helps people feel less overwhelmed and more in control.

Good communication also means knowing how to talk to different kinds of people. A social worker might speak gently to a child who's scared or use encour-aging words with someone who feels stuck. They might talk calmly to someone who's upset, helping them feel heard instead of judged. Communication isn't just about talking—it's about connecting with people in a way that makes them feel valued.

Sometimes, social workers have to bring people together to solve problems. Imagine a neighborhood that wants a new playground. The social worker might organize a meeting with parents, kids, and city offi-cials. They'd need to listen to everyone's ideas, explain the steps to get the playground built, and make sure everyone works as a team. This kind of communication takes patience and the ability to see things from different perspectives.

All these skills—listening, empathy, problem-solving, and communication—work together like the gears in a machine. A social worker might start by listening to someone's story, using empathy to understand how they feel. Then they'd use problem-solving to come up with solutions and communication to explain those solutions clearly. Each skill builds on the others, helping the social worker do their job effectively.

Traits needed

Being kind isn't just about smiling or saying nice things; it's about caring deeply for others and wanting to make their lives better. Social workers often meet people who feel hopeless, scared, or alone. Imagine a girl named Emma who's being bullied at school. She doesn't feel safe talking to anyone about it. When Emma finally tells her social worker, she's met with kindness instead of judgment. That kindness makes her feel safe enough to share more, which is the first step toward finding a solution.

Kindness isn't always easy, especially when the

person being helped is angry or upset. Take a father named Carlos who's struggling to find work. He feels embarrassed and frustrated, and when he talks to a social worker, his anger bubbles over. Instead of snapping back, the social worker responds with kindness, understanding that Carlos's anger comes from fear and stress. By staying calm and caring, the social worker helps Carlos feel heard and respected, which opens the door to finding solutions together.

Patience is another trait every social worker needs. Helping people isn't always quick or simple. Sometimes it takes weeks, months, or even years to see progress. Imagine a family who's trying to rebuild their life after losing their home in a fire. They need to find a new place to live, replace their belongings, and heal emotionally. The social worker supporting them has to be patient, knowing that progress will come step by step. Patience helps the social worker stay focused, even when things move slowly.

Patience also comes in handy when plans don't work out the first time. Imagine a social worker helping a teenager named Noah, who's trying to quit skipping school. They agree on a plan to improve Noah's attendance, but he skips class again the next week. Instead of giving up, the social worker shows patience, sitting down with Noah to figure out why the plan didn't work and how they can adjust it. Patience means sticking with someone even when the road gets bumpy.

Determination is just as important. Social workers often face challenges that seem overwhelming, like helping families find housing when there aren't enough affordable homes available. Determination means not giving up, even when the odds are stacked against them. Imagine a mom named Latoya who's been on a waiting list for an apartment for months. Her social worker keeps calling housing agencies, filling out forms, and looking for other options, refusing to give up until Latoya has a safe place to live. That kind of determination can change lives.

Determination also helps social workers keep going when their work feels exhausting. Think about a community that's recovering from a hurricane. The social worker there might be working long hours, coordinating supplies, finding shelter for families, and comforting people who've lost everything. It's hard work, but determination keeps them going, knowing that their efforts are making a difference.

Finally, there's a strong sense of fairness. Social workers believe that everyone deserves the same chance to succeed, no matter who they are or where they come from. Imagine a boy named Liam who has a disability and feels left out at school because he can't join in the same activities as his classmates. His social worker helps create a plan to make the school more inclusive, like adding ramps for his wheelchair or finding ways for him to participate in gym class. That's fairness in action—making sure Liam gets the same opportunities as everyone else.

Fairness also means standing up for people who might not have a voice. Imagine a community where some families don't have access to clean drinking water because of old, broken pipes. A social worker might organize a meeting with local leaders, speaking up for those families and pushing for changes to fix the problem. By fighting for fairness, the social worker helps create a better future for the entire community.

What ties these traits together is a deep belief in the value of every person. Social workers don't see their work as fixing people; they see it as helping people find their strength and overcome challenges. Whether it's showing kindness to someone who feels invisible, practicing patience during tough times, staying determined when solutions seem far away, or standing up for fairness, social workers bring these traits to every situation they face.

Problem Solving Activity

Imagine you're sitting at lunch with a friend who looks upset. They're poking at their food and staring out the window, not saying much. Finally, they tell you what's wrong—they forgot to do their math homework, and now they're worried about getting in trouble with the teacher. What would you do? Would you listen and try to cheer them up? Maybe you'd help them come up with a plan to finish their homework after lunch or offer to study with them later. Solving a problem like this might seem small, but it uses the same skills and traits social workers rely on every day.

Let's take a closer look at what it takes to solve problems for friends, family, or even yourself. Each step is like putting together the pieces of a puzzle— every piece counts, and when they all fit together, you create a solution.

Start with listening. When your friend tells you they're upset about their math homework, what's the first thing you do? You probably stop what you're doing and give them your full attention. Maybe you lean in, nod, or say something like, "That sounds stressful." By listening carefully, you show your friend that you care about what they're feeling. You might even notice details that help you understand the problem better, like if they seem more worried about disappointing the teacher than about the homework itself. Listening isn't just about hearing words; it's about understanding the emotions behind them.

Next, think about showing empathy. Imagine how you'd feel if you were in your friend's shoes. Maybe you'd feel nervous, embarrassed, or frustrated. By imagining what they're going through, you can respond in a way that makes them feel supported. You might say, "I'd feel the same way if I were you. Math homework can be really hard." Empathy helps your friend feel understood, which is an important part of solving the problem together.

Now comes the brainstorming part. This is where problem-solving skills come in. What could help your friend fix the situation? Maybe they could explain to the teacher that they forgot the homework but promise to finish it by the end of the day. Or maybe they could ask for help with the parts they don't understand. Brainstorming is about coming up with as many ideas as possible, even if some of them seem a little silly at first. The more options you have, the easier it is to find one that works.

Once you have a few ideas, it's time to choose the best one. This is where good communication comes into play. You might say, "How do you feel about talking to the teacher? Do you think that would help?" Asking questions like this makes your friend part of the decision, which helps them feel more confident about trying the solution. Communication is also about being clear. If your friend isn't sure how to approach the teacher, you could help them practice what to say.

Imagine you're helping a younger sibling instead of a friend. Let's say your sibling is upset because they lost their favorite toy. First, you'd listen to them explain what happened. Maybe they say they last saw it in the living room but now it's gone. Then you'd show empathy by saying, "That must be so frustrating! I'd be upset if I lost my favorite toy too." Next, you'd start brainstorming ways to find it. Maybe you check under the couch, retrace their steps, or ask other family members if they've seen it. Finally, you'd choose a plan and put it into action—like helping your sibling search every room in the house. Even if it takes time, your patience and kindness make the process easier for them.

Sometimes the problem isn't about fixing something but about helping someone feel better. Imagine your cousin is nervous about performing in a school play. They tell you they're afraid of forgetting their lines. You listen to their worries, showing empathy by saying, "It's totally normal to feel nervous before a big performance." Then you brainstorm ways to help them feel more prepared. Maybe you offer to practice lines with them or remind them that everyone in the audience wants them to do well. By being patient and encouraging, you help your cousin build the confidence they need.

Now let's think about a group problem. Imagine your classmates are arguing about who gets to play goalie during soccer practice. Everyone is frustrated, and no one can agree. How would you solve this? First, you'd listen to each person's side of the story. Maybe one person says they always play goalie, while another says they've never had a chance. Showing empathy means recognizing that both sides have valid feelings. You might say, "I can see why you're upset. You really want a turn, and you really like being the goalie." Then you'd brainstorm a fair solution. Could they take turns? Could one person play goalie this time and the other next time? Problem-solving in groups often involves finding a compromise that works for everyone.

Sometimes, solving problems means asking for help. Imagine your best friend is having a tough time at home and tells you they feel really sad all the time. This is a big problem, and you might not have all the answers. That's okay! Showing kindness and empathy means listening to your friend and letting them know it's brave to share their feelings. Then you could suggest they talk to an adult they trust, like a parent, teacher, or school counselor. Asking for help is an important part of solving big problems because it brings in people who have the experience and resources to make a difference.

4

THE PATH TO BECOMING A SOCIAL WORKER

The journey to becoming a social worker starts in high school. You might not realize it, but the subjects you're studying now can help you build the foundation you'll need later. For example, classes like English and history teach you how to understand stories and communicate clearly, both of which are important for social workers. Science classes, like biology or psychology, can help you understand how people's minds and bodies work, which is useful when you're helping others.

Imagine you're in a psychology class, learning about how people think and behave. You might study why some people feel anxious or how kids develop different skills as they grow. These lessons give you a better understanding of the challenges people face and how to support them. Even math can come in handy for social workers, especially if you're helping families with budgets or organizing community programs.

Beyond academics, high school is also a great time to start developing the traits social workers need, like kindness, patience, and determination. Maybe you volunteer at a local food bank or join a club that helps your community. These experiences teach you how to work with others and make a difference, even in small ways.

After high school, the next step is college. Most social workers earn a bachelor's degree, which usually takes about four years. This is where you dive deeper into the knowledge and skills needed for the job. Many social workers major in social work, psychology, or sociology. These fields focus on understanding people, communities, and the systems that shape our lives.

Imagine you're a college student studying social work. One of your classes might focus on learning how to listen to people and understand their needs. Another might teach you about social justice and how to fight for fairness in your community. You might also learn about different cultures and how to work with people from all backgrounds. Each class adds another piece to the puzzle, helping you become a better social worker.

In college, you'll also have opportunities to get hands-on experience. Many social work programs include internships, where you work with real social workers to help people in your community. For example, you might spend a semester helping kids at an after-school program or visiting patients in a hospital. These experiences let you practice what you've learned in class while seeing the difference social workers make firsthand.

After earning a bachelor's degree, some social workers decide to continue their education by earning a master's degree. This step isn't always required, but it can open up more opportunities, especially if you want to work in specialized areas like therapy or leadership roles. A master's degree usually takes about two years and allows you to focus on specific topics, like mental health, child welfare, or community organizing.

Imagine you're in a master's program, studying advanced ways to help people. You might learn how to create programs that support families in need or how to counsel someone going through a tough time. You'd also spend more time working in the field, learning from experienced social workers and building your confidence.

Education for social workers doesn't stop when you finish school. Social workers are always learning, whether it's through workshops, conferences, or reading about new research. Imagine a social worker attending a workshop about using technology to help people in rural areas. They might learn about apps that connect people to resources or ways to offer counseling online. This kind of learning helps social workers stay up-to-date and find new ways to make a difference.

Important subjects in school

Think about the subjects you learn in school: math, science, history, English. Each one helps you understand the world in a different way. But did you know that some of these subjects are especially important for social workers? Psychology, sociology, and communication are like the building blocks for understanding people and solving problems. If you've ever been curious about why people think the way they do, how societies work, or how to connect with others, these are the subjects where those questions start to take shape.

Let's start with psychology. At its heart, psychology is the study of how people think, feel, and behave. Imagine you're learning about why some people feel really happy one day and really sad the next. That's psychology. Social workers often help people who are struggling with their emotions or dealing with tough situations, and understanding psychology gives them the tools to do that.

Picture a kid named Zoe who's having trouble making friends at school. She feels nervous talking to new people and sometimes stays quiet even when she wants to join in. A social worker who's studied psychology might understand that Zoe's nervousness could come from something called social anxiety. With that knowledge, the social worker could help Zoe learn ways to feel more confident and practice talking to others. Psychology helps social workers see what's happening beneath the surface and find ways to support people like Zoe.

Psychology also helps social workers understand how people grow and change over time. Imagine learning about why babies cry to get attention or why teenagers sometimes push boundaries. These are all part of human development, a topic that social workers study to better understand the people they help. Knowing what's normal for different stages of life helps social workers figure out when someone might need extra support.

Now let's talk about sociology. While psychology focuses on individuals, sociology looks at groups, communities, and societies. It's the study of how people interact with each other and how things like culture, family, and social rules shape our lives. Imagine learning about why certain traditions are important in some cultures or how families in different parts of the world live and work together. That's sociology.

Social workers use sociology to understand the bigger picture. Imagine a neighborhood where many families are struggling to find good jobs. A social worker who's studied sociology might look at how the local economy, education system, or transportation options are affecting those families. Instead of just helping one family at a time, they could work on solutions that help the whole community, like organizing job training programs or advocating for better public transportation. Sociology helps social workers see how problems are connected and think about solutions that make a big impact.

Sociology also helps social workers understand diversity and inclusion. People come from all kinds of backgrounds, and what works for one person might not work for someone else. Imagine meeting someone who speaks a different language or celebrates different holidays. Sociology teaches social workers to approach each person with respect and curiosity, asking, "What's important to you?" and "How can I support you in a way that makes sense for your life?" This kind of understanding builds trust and helps social workers connect with the people they're helping.

Communication is the third key subject for social workers, and it's all about how people share information and understand each other. Good communication is more than just talking—it's listening, reading body language, and choosing words that make people feel safe and understood. Imagine sitting with someone who's nervous or upset. The way you speak, the tone of your voice, and even the way you sit can help them feel more comfortable.

Think about a teenager named Jordan who's arguing with his parents about staying out late. Jordan is frustrated, and his parents are worried. A social worker might use communication skills to help both sides feel heard. They might say to Jordan, "It sounds like you want more freedom because you feel ready to handle it," and to his parents, "I hear that you're concerned about Jordan's safety." By reflecting what each person is feeling, the social worker helps everyone feel understood, which makes it easier to find a solution.

Communication also helps social workers explain complicated ideas in simple ways. Imagine trying to describe how health insurance works to someone who's never used it before. A social worker might break it down step by step, using examples to make it easier to understand. Clear communication helps people feel less overwhelmed and more in control of their choices.

Another part of communication is working with groups. Imagine a social worker leading a meeting with parents, teachers, and kids to plan a new after-school program. They'd need to listen to everyone's ideas, explain the steps to get the program started, and help the group work together. This kind of communication takes patience, creativity, and the ability to see things from different perspectives.

What makes these subjects so important is how they fit together. Psychology helps social workers understand what's going on inside a person's mind. Sociology helps them ee how communities and cultures shape people's experiences. Communication ties it all together, allowing social workers to connect with others and share ideas clearly. Together, these subjects give social workers the tools they need to make a difference.

Internships and volunteering

When someone is studying social work in college, they spend a lot of time in classrooms learning about psychology, sociology, and communication. These subjects teach them important concepts, but the real magic happens when they step out into the world and start applying those lessons. Internships and volunteering give future social workers a chance to see the challenges and rewards of the job up close.

Think about a college student named Maya. She's studying to become a social worker and decides to volunteer at a local homeless shelter. At first, she's nervous. She's read about homelessness in her classes, but now she's meeting people who are living it every day. Maya starts by helping serve meals, listening to the guests' stories, and working with the staff to connect people to housing programs. Over time, she learns how to handle difficult situations, like when someone feels frustrated or hopeless. Volunteering at the shelter helps Maya realize that social work isn't just about knowing facts—it's about building relationships and showing compassion.

Internships work in a similar way, but they're often more structured and connected to a college program. Imagine a student named Jordan who's doing an internship at a hospital. Jordan's job is to shadow a hospital social worker, which means following them around and watching how they do their work. One day, they might meet with a patient who's worried about paying their medical bills. The next, they might help a family understand a loved one's diagnosis. Jordan doesn't just watch—he gets to help, too. Maybe he makes phone calls to find resources for a patient or explains a hospital program to a family. Each task gives Jordan valuable experience and shows him what it's like to be a social worker in a busy, high-pressure environment.

One of the best things about internships and volunteering is that they let future social workers try different types of work. Social work isn't just one job—it's many. Some social workers help kids in schools, while others support elderly people, families, or communities. By volunteering or interning in different places, students can figure out what kind of social work feels like the best fit for them.

Take Sophia, for example. She thought she wanted to work with families, so she signed up for an internship at a family services agency. But during her internship, she realized she really enjoyed working with teenagers who were figuring out their next steps after high school. After that, she decided to focus on youth programs instead. Internships and volunteering are like trying on different hats—they help students discover what feels right.

These experiences aren't just about learning skills —they're also about making connections. When students work or volunteer in real-world settings, they meet social workers who have been doing the job for years. These experienced professionals can offer advice, share stories, and even become mentors. Imagine a student named Alex who's volunteering at a community center. One of the social workers there notices that Alex has a great way of connecting with kids and gives him tips on how to handle tough conversations. That advice helps Alex feel more confident and ready for his future career.

Sometimes, internships and volunteering teach students about challenges they didn't expect. Imagine working at a shelter where not everyone is ready to accept help. Some people might feel scared, others might be angry, and some might not know what kind of help they need. These moments can be hard, but they also teach future social workers the importance of patience and perseverance. They learn that change doesn't always happen overnight, but every small step matters.

Volunteering can start long before college. Even middle school or high school students can find ways to help their communities. Imagine organizing a food drive, visiting a nursing home, or helping out at a local animal shelter. These activities might not seem directly related to social work, but they build the same skills: listening, problem-solving, and understanding what people need. They also show that making a difference doesn't require a degree—it starts with caring.

Internships and volunteering also help students see the impact of their work. Imagine helping a family find a safe place to live or supporting a teenager as they overcome a tough challenge. These moments remind future social workers why they chose this path in the first place. It's not always easy, but seeing someone smile or hearing a heartfelt thank-you makes it all worth it.

5

CHALLENGES SOCIAL WORKERS FACE

One of the hardest parts of being a social worker is balancing emotions. Imagine working with a family that's just lost their home in a fire. They're scared, overwhelmed, and don't know what to do next. As a social worker, you'd want to help them figure out their next steps, like finding a temporary place to stay or applying for assistance. But at the same time, you'd also feel their sadness and worry. It's natural to care deeply, but if you take on all their emotions, it can start to feel like carrying that heavy backpack.

TO BALANCE THEIR EMOTIONS, social workers learn how to care without letting the weight of every problem overwhelm them. One way they do this is by focusing on the things they can do. Imagine sitting with a family after something difficult has happened. You might not be able to fix everything, but you can offer comfort and guidance. That's what social workers remind themselves—small steps can make a big difference.

ANOTHER WAY social workers manage their emotions is by talking to others. Just like you might tell a friend about a tough day at school, social workers talk to their coworkers or supervisors when they're feeling overwhelmed. They share their feelings in a safe and private way, which helps them process what they're going through. It's not about complaining—it's about finding support so they can keep helping others.

LET'S picture a social worker named Sam who works at a hospital. One day, Sam meets a young boy named Ethan who's been in a car accident. Ethan's leg is broken, and he's scared about whether he'll be able to play soccer again. Sam talks to Ethan and his parents, helping them understand the recovery process and connect with physical therapy. While Sam feels good about helping Ethan, it's also hard to see him in pain. Later, Sam talks to a colleague, sharing how difficult it was to see Ethan upset. By talking it through, Sam feels less alone and more ready to keep helping.

SOMETIMES, social workers also need to take care of themselves. Imagine trying to help others when you're tired, stressed, or feeling down—it's much harder to be there for someone else if you're not feeling your best. Social workers practice self-care, which means doing things that help them recharge and feel balanced. That might be something simple, like going for a walk, spending time with friends, or reading a favorite book. Taking time for themselves helps social workers stay strong and focused.

THINK about a social worker named Elena who works with families in a busy city. Her days are filled with meeting people, making phone calls, and solving problems. Sometimes it feels there's not enough time to do everything, and Elena starts to feel stressed. She decides to set aside 30 minutes every evening to do something relaxing, like painting or listening to music. That small act of self-care makes a big difference, helping her feel calmer and ready for the next day.

ANOTHER CHALLENGE social workers face is knowing they can't fix everything. Imagine helping a student named Jordan who's struggling with school and family problems. You do everything you can to support him —talking to his teachers, helping his parents find resources, and checking in regularly. But even with all that help, Jordan still has tough days. Social workers learn that they can't solve every problem, but they can still make a difference by being there and doing their best.

IT'S ALSO important for social workers to remember the successes. While some days are hard, other days bring moments of joy and progress. Imagine a social worker named Priya who's been helping a family find a new home after being in a shelter. One day, Priya gets a call from the family, telling her they've moved into their new house. Hearing their excitement and gratitude reminds Priya why she became a social worker in the first place.

Challenges Social Workers Face

Imagine a social worker named Ms. Taylor who works with a boy named Liam. Liam is 10 years old, and his family is struggling to afford food and rent. Liam over-heard his parents talking about money and is now worried about whether they'll have a place to live. When he asks Ms. Taylor, "Are we going to lose our house?" she knows she needs to answer carefully.

Ms. Taylor might start by acknowledging Liam's feelings. "It sounds like you're feeling worried about what you heard," she might say. "That's okay—it's normal to feel this way when you don't know what's going to happen." Then, she'd explain the situation in simple terms, without adding unnecessary fear. "Your family is going through a hard time right now, and money is tight. But we're working on finding ways to help, like making sure there's food and keeping your home safe." By focusing on what's being done to help, Ms. Taylor reassures Liam while also being truthful.

Another challenge social workers face is explaining illness, especially when it affects someone a child loves. Imagine a social worker named Mr. Rivera working with an 8-year-old girl named Sofia. Sofia's mom has been diagnosed with cancer, and she doesn't fully understand what that means. She asks Mr. Rivera, "Is my mom going to get better?"

MR. RIVERA KNOWS this is a tough question. He starts by asking Sofia what she already knows. "Can you tell me what you've noticed about your mom lately?" he might say. Sofia explains that her mom has been very tired and hasn't been able to play with her like she used to. Mr. Rivera listens carefully, then explains the situation using simple, age-appropriate language. "Your mom is sick right now, and her body is working really hard to fight the sickness. The doctors are doing everything they can to help her get better, and she's taking medicine to make her stronger. It might take time, but there are lots of people helping her."

BY FOCUSING on what's happening now and avoiding making promises about the future, Mr. Rivera helps Sofia understand her mom's illness without giving her false hope.

. . .

SOMETIMES SOCIAL WORKERS need to explain situations that involve changes in a family, like when parents get divorced or when a child is placed in foster care. Imagine a social worker named Ms. Chen talking to a boy named Ethan, whose parents are divorcing. Ethan feels confused and blames himself for their arguments.

MS. CHEN STARTS by reassuring Ethan that the divorce isn't his fault. "Sometimes grown-ups have problems that they need to work out, and those problems aren't because of anything you did," she says gently. She then explains the changes in a way that helps Ethan understand what to expect. "You'll still see both of your parents, but they'll be living in different houses. They both love you very much, and they're working together to make sure you're okay."

BY FOCUSING on the facts and offering reassurance, Ms. Chen helps Ethan feel less scared about what's happening.

.   .   .

EXPLAINING POVERTY, illness, or family changes isn't just about finding the right words—it's also about understanding how kids think and feel. Younger children might focus on how a situation affects their daily routine, while older kids might ask deeper questions about why things happen. Social workers adjust their explanations based on what each child needs.

IMAGINE a 7-year-old named Bella who notices her classmate doesn't always bring lunch to school. Bella asks her social worker, Mr. Parker, why that happens. Mr. Parker explains in a simple way, saying, "Sometimes families don't have enough money to buy all the food they need. That's why schools have programs to help, like giving free lunches to kids who need them."

NOW IMAGINE AN OLDER KID, like 12-year-old Jamal, asking why some families are poor while others aren't. Mr. Parker might give a broader explanation, saying, "There are many reasons why families struggle with money. Some people don't have jobs, or their jobs don't pay enough. Sometimes it's because of things like expensive bills or emergencies that are hard to handle. It's not fair, which is why people and programs try to help."

How social workers handle stress

Stress is a normal part of life, and it's especially common in jobs where people help others. Social workers face a lot of difficult situations, like helping families who don't have enough food, supporting kids whose parents are divorcing, or finding resources for someone who's sick. These challenges can feel heavy, and if a social worker doesn't handle their stress, it can start to affect how they think, feel, and work.

ONE WAY social workers handle stress is by taking breaks. Imagine trying to solve a really hard puzzle without stepping away for a moment. Sometimes, your brain needs a rest to come back stronger. Social workers do this by scheduling time to step back from their work. Maybe they go for a walk during lunch, spend time with friends after a busy day, or take a weekend off to recharge. These small breaks give them the energy they need to keep helping others.

.   .   .

THINK about a social worker named Mr. Davis, who works at a hospital. His days are full of meetings with patients and their families, solving problems, and helping people through difficult times. After work, Mr. Davis likes to go to a local park and walk along the trails. Being outside in nature helps him feel calm and clears his mind. It's his way of recharging after a long day.

ANOTHER WAY social workers handle stress is by talking about their feelings. Imagine carrying a heavy backpack—it feels lighter when someone helps you hold it, right? For social workers, sharing their thoughts and emotions with someone they trust makes a big difference. They might talk to a friend, a family member, or another social worker who understands what they're going through. These conversations don't solve every problem, but they make the load feel a little easier to carry.

SOMETIMES, social workers even work with counselors or therapists themselves. It might sound surprising that people who help others would need help too, but it's actually very common. Just like a doctor might go to another doctor when they're sick, social workers know it's important to take care of their mental health.

Social workers also use something called mindfulness to handle stress. Mindfulness means paying attention to the present moment and letting go of worries about the past or future. Imagine sitting quietly and focusing on your breathing, or noticing the sounds around you, like birds chirping or leaves rustling in the wind. These small moments of calm help social workers feel more centered and less over-whelmed.

Think about Ms. Patel, a social worker who helps kids in foster care. Her job is full of big emotions—she's there when kids feel scared, angry, or sad. To handle her stress, Ms. Patel spends a few minutes each morning practicing mindfulness. She sits quietly, breathes deeply, and reminds herself why her work is important. It helps her start the day feeling focused and ready.

.   .   .

EXERCISE IS another way social workers stay healthy. Moving your body can do wonders for your mood and energy levels, whether it's running, swimming, or even dancing around your room. Social workers often make time for activities that keep them active and help them feel good. It's not just about staying fit—it's about releasing the stress that builds up during the day.

IMAGINE A SOCIAL WORKER NAMED CARLOS, who loves playing basketball. After a long week of work, he meets up with friends at the community center for a game. Running up and down the court, laughing with his friends, and making a few good shots all help Carlos shake off the stress of his week.

EATING healthy food and getting enough sleep are also important. Think about how tired you feel after staying up too late or how sluggish you feel after eating too much junk food. Social workers know that taking care of their bodies helps them handle the challenges of their job. They make time to eat meals that give them energy and to rest when they need it.

. . .

ANOTHER WAY social workers stay healthy is by focusing on what they can control. They know they can't fix every problem or make everyone's life perfect, but they can take small steps that make a big difference. By setting realistic goals and celebrating small successes, they remind themselves that their work matters, even when it feels tough.

THINK about a social worker named Elena, who helps families find housing. She knows she can't solve the housing crisis overnight, but she focuses on helping one family at a time. When a family moves into a new apartment, Elena feels proud of the part she played in making it happen. That sense of accomplishment helps her stay motivated.

FINALLY, social workers surround themselves with things that bring them joy. Maybe it's listening to music, reading a good book, or spending time with a pet. These small moments of happiness remind them that life is about balance—there's room for both hard work and fun.

6

REWARDS OF BEING A SOCIAL WORKER

Helping people isn't always easy, but the moments when you see someone smile, feel more confident, or succeed after struggling make all the hard work worth it. For social workers, these moments are what keep them going.

Take Ms. Rivera, a school social worker who helps students like Jamal, a shy 12-year-old struggling with making friends. Jamal often ate lunch alone and felt left out during recess. Ms. Rivera worked with Jamal, helping him find ways to start conversations and join in games. She also talked to his teacher about pairing him with classmates who shared his interests.

Weeks later, Ms. Rivera watched Jamal laughing with a group of kids on the playground. That moment made her heart swell with pride. She didn't just see a boy playing—she saw the results of her efforts to help him feel more confident. Knowing she made a difference in Jamal's life brought her an incredible sense of satisfaction.

Social workers don't always see immediate results, but when they do, it's like watching a seed they planted grow into a strong, healthy tree. Imagine Mr. Lee, a community social worker who worked with families in a neighborhood that didn't have a safe place for kids to play. He spent months organizing meetings, talking to city officials, and rallying neighbors to create a new park.

The day the park opened, Mr. Lee stood at the edge of the playground, watching kids climb the jungle gym and swing on the swings. Parents sat on benches, chatting while keeping an eye on their kids. Seeing the joy and sense of community the park brought made Mr. Lee feel like all his hard work had paid off.

The personal satisfaction of helping people isn't just about big, life-changing moments. Sometimes it's in the small, quiet victories. Imagine Ms. Patel, a hospital social worker, sitting with a patient who's just been diagnosed with a serious illness. The patient feels scared and overwhelmed, but as Ms. Patel listens and talks with them, they begin to feel calmer.

Later, the patient thanks Ms. Patel, saying, "You made me feel like I wasn't alone." Those words stay with her long after the day is over. Even though she couldn't change the patient's diagnosis, she made a difference by being there and offering comfort.

For social workers, every person they help is a reminder of why they chose this path. Each story of someone overcoming a challenge or finding hope is like a spark that keeps their passion alive.

Think about Mr. Carter, who works with kids in foster care. One of the boys he helped, Jason, had been in and out of several foster homes and was struggling to trust adults. Mr. Carter spent months building a relationship with Jason, helping him feel safe and supported.

One day, Jason was placed with a foster family who truly cared for him, and he began to thrive. At a school event, Jason introduced Mr. Carter to his foster parents, saying, "This is the guy who helped me believe things could get better." Hearing those words filled Mr. Carter with pride and joy, reminding him of the power of his work.

Social workers often find that the people they help also inspire them. Imagine Ms. Thompson, who supports families facing poverty. She worked with a single mom, Latoya, who was determined to create a better life for her kids. Despite working two jobs and going back to school, Latoya always found time to show love and care for her children.

Watching Latoya's determination and strength inspired Ms. Thompson to work even harder to find resources for the family. When Latoya graduated from her program and got a better job, she thanked Ms. Thompson for her support. But Ms. Thompson felt just as grateful for Latoya, whose resilience reminded her why her work mattered.

Helping others also teaches social workers important life lessons. They learn to appreciate small victories, to celebrate progress even when it's slow, and to find joy in connection. Imagine Mr. Daniels, a social worker in a retirement home. His job involves helping residents adjust to their new surroundings and cope with loneliness.

One resident, Mr. Harris, had been feeling isolated since moving in. Mr. Daniels helped him join a gardening club at the home, and over time, Mr. Harris became one of the most active members. Seeing Mr. Harris smile as he shared tips with other residents in the garden gave Mr. Daniels a deep sense of fulfillment.

Social workers also experience the satisfaction of knowing they're part of something bigger. Every time they help someone, they're contributing to a ripple effect of kindness and change. A child who gains confidence might grow up to help others. A family who finds stability might give back to their community.

For Ms. Nguyen, a social worker who runs parenting workshops, this ripple effect is clear. One mom, Maria, came to her workshops feeling unsure about how to handle her kids' tantrums. Over several sessions, Maria learned new strategies and began to feel more confident.

Months later, Maria returned to the workshop—not as a participant, but as a guest speaker, sharing her story to inspire other parents. Seeing Maria pass on what she had learned filled Ms. Nguyen with pride, knowing she had played a role in creating a positive cycle of support.

Making a lasting difference in someone's life

Imagine planting a tiny seed in the ground. At first, it doesn't look like much is happening. You water it, give it sunlight, and protect it from harsh weather. Slowly, almost without you noticing, the seed begins to grow. One day, it blooms into a strong, beautiful tree that offers shade and shelter for years to come. That's what it's like for social workers when they make a lasting difference in someone's life. They might not see the results right away, but their efforts can change someone's life forever.

Take the story of Mr. Lewis, a social worker at a youth center. He met a teenager named Kai, who had just moved to the area and was struggling to fit in at school. Kai felt invisible, like no one cared about him. Mr. Lewis saw how talented Kai was at drawing and encouraged him to join an art class at the center. At first, Kai was shy, but with Mr. Lewis cheering him on, he started to open up.

Years later, Kai came back to the youth center—not as a participant, but as a guest speaker. He was now a successful graphic designer and wanted to inspire other kids to follow their passions. He told the group, "Mr. Lewis believed in me when I didn't believe in myself. That changed everything for me."

For Mr. Lewis, hearing those words was one of the greatest rewards of his career. He didn't just help Kai for a moment; he planted a seed of confidence that grew into something amazing.

Making a lasting difference isn't always about grand gestures. Sometimes it's the small, consistent acts of kindness that stay with people. Imagine Ms. Carter, a school social worker who worked with a boy named Jaden. Jaden often got in trouble for not paying attention in class, but Ms. Carter noticed he was really curious about how things worked. She arranged for Jaden to spend time with the school's maintenance team, learning how they fixed things.

Jaden loved it. He discovered he had a knack for repairing and building. By the time he finished high school, he had a clear goal: to become an engineer. Years later, Jaden sent Ms. Carter a letter thanking her for helping him find his path.

That letter reminded Ms. Carter of the ripple effect of her work. By helping Jaden discover his talents, she hadn't just changed his life—she had also set him on a path to contribute to the world in his own unique way.

Sometimes, making a lasting difference means being there during someone's hardest moments. Imagine Mr. Patel, a social worker at a hospital, meeting a woman named Nina who had just lost her husband. Nina was overwhelmed with grief and unsure how to move forward. Mr. Patel listened to her, connected her with a support group, and encouraged her to take things one step at a time.

A year later, Nina returned to the hospital—not as a patient, but as a volunteer for the same support group that had helped her. She told Mr. Patel, "You gave me hope when I didn't think I'd ever feel okay again. I want to do that for others now."

For Mr. Patel, seeing Nina help others was a powerful reminder of the impact of his work. He didn't just help her through a tough time—he helped her find strength she didn't know she had, and now she was passing that strength on to others.

Social workers often make a lasting difference by helping people believe in themselves. Imagine Ms. Lee, a family social worker, working with a single mom named Rosa who was struggling to provide for her two kids. Rosa felt like she was failing, but Ms. Lee reminded her of how hard she was working and helped her find resources to get back on her feet.

A few years later, Rosa started her own small business and became a mentor for other single moms in her community. When Ms. Lee visited Rosa's business, she saw photos of Rosa and her kids, smiling and thriving. Rosa said, "You helped me see that I could do this. Now I want to help others see it too."

Moments like these remind social workers that their efforts have lasting effects. They're not just solving problems—they're empowering people to create their own solutions.

Making a lasting difference also happens when social workers inspire others to care. Think about Mr.

Daniels, a community social worker who organized a neighborhood clean-up. At first, only a few people showed up, but by the end of the day, the neighborhood looked better, and people felt proud of what they'd accomplished together.

Over the next few months, more people started getting involved, organizing events and supporting each other. What started as a simple clean-up became a movement to create a stronger, kinder community. Mr. Daniels smiled as he walked through the neighborhood, seeing the changes and knowing he had played a part in bringing people together.

7

HOW KIDS CAN HELP NOW

One of the easiest ways to help is by donating toys or clothes you no longer use. Imagine another kid opening a box and finding a teddy bear or a cool puzzle that makes their day brighter. Maybe you have a toy you've outgrown, but it's still in great condition. Instead of letting it gather dust, you could donate it to a local shelter or charity. Not only does it clear space in your room, but it also brings joy to someone else.

Think about Emma, who decided to go through her toys one weekend. She found a dollhouse she hadn't played with in years. Emma cleaned it up, packed it carefully, and took it to a community center that supports families in need. A few weeks later, Emma saw a picture of a little girl playing with the dollhouse, her face lit up with happiness. That small action made a big impact.

If donating toys sounds fun, you can take it a step further by organizing a collection drive. Maybe you and your friends could gather school supplies, books, or canned food to donate. Imagine setting up a table at school with a sign that says "Help Us Help Others!" People could drop off items, and you'd be the ones delivering them to local organizations. It's like being a superhero team for your community.

Another way to help is by volunteering with your family. Volunteering doesn't mean doing something huge or complicated—it's about giving your time and effort to help others. Imagine spending a morning at an animal shelter, helping to walk dogs or play with cats. Or maybe your family could volunteer at a food bank, packing boxes of groceries for people who need them.

Ethan and his mom spent a Saturday at a park clean-up event. They wore gloves, picked up litter, and even planted flowers. At first, Ethan thought it might be boring, but by the end of the day, he felt proud seeing how much better the park looked. The best part? People walking by stopped to thank him, which made him feel like he'd done something really important.

Sometimes, helping can be as simple as being kind to your neighbors. Imagine an elderly neighbor who has trouble carrying groceries. Offering to help them could make their day. Or maybe your neighbor just got a new puppy and could use an extra hand walking it. These small acts of kindness show that you care, and they make your community stronger.

Another idea is to support local causes. Have you ever seen a bake sale or a lemonade stand raising money for a good cause? You could organize something similar. Imagine baking cookies with your friends, decorating a sign, and selling treats to raise money for a local animal rescue or library. Every dollar helps, and it's a fun way to bring people together.

Think about Mia and her soccer team, who decided to raise money for a new playground in their town. They set up a car wash and charged just a few dollars per car. By the end of the day, they had raised enough money to make a big contribution to the project. Now, whenever Mia sees kids playing on the playground, she feels proud knowing she helped make it happen.

If you're someone who loves art or writing, you can use your creativity to help others. Imagine making cheerful cards for people in a hospital or writing letters to soldiers far from home. These small gestures remind people that someone is thinking about them, which can make a huge difference.

Leila, who loves drawing, started creating colorful bookmarks to give to her local library. She decorated them with encouraging messages like "You're Amazing!" and "Keep Smiling!" The librarian loved them so much that she handed them out to kids checking out books. Leila was thrilled to see her art spreading positivity.

Helping the environment is another way to make a difference. Imagine planting a tree in your backyard or organizing a recycling program at school. Even simple actions, like picking up trash during a walk or switching to reusable water bottles, can help protect the planet. You're not just helping people—you're helping the Earth.

Daniel decided to start a composting project in his backyard. He learned how to turn food scraps into soil and taught his neighbors to do the same. Over time, the whole block started composting, which reduced waste and helped their gardens grow. Daniel felt like he was part of something much bigger than himself.

If you're passionate about helping animals, you could organize a pet supply drive for a local shelter. Imagine collecting blankets, toys, or pet food to donate. Or, if you have a pet at home, you could teach younger kids how to care for animals by sharing tips or hosting a mini "pet care workshop."

Helping doesn't always mean big projects. Sometimes, it's about paying attention to the people around you. Imagine noticing that a classmate looks sad and sitting with them at lunch. Or helping a younger sibling with homework. These small acts of kindness show people they're not alone, which is one of the best ways to make a difference.

Empathy and kindness in everyday life.

Empathy means putting yourself in someone else's shoes and trying to understand how they feel. Imagine a classmate who looks upset because they didn't do well on a test. You might feel tempted to move on with your day, but stopping to say, "I'm sorry you're feeling down—do you want to talk about it?" can make them feel less alone. That's empathy in action: noticing when someone is struggling and showing that you care.

Think about a boy named Liam who noticed his friend Maya was unusually quiet during recess. Instead of ignoring it, Liam asked her, "Are you okay? You seem a little sad today." Maya explained that she

was worried about her dog, who was sick. Liam didn't
have to fix the problem, but just listening and showing
he cared made Maya feel better. Later, she thanked
him, saying, "It really helped to talk about it."

Kindness goes hand in hand with empathy. It's
about doing something thoughtful to make someone
else's day a little better. Imagine holding the door
open for someone carrying a heavy backpack, sharing
your snack with a friend who forgot theirs, or writing
a thank-you note to your teacher. These small gestures
might seem simple, but they show people that you
care about them.

Take Emma, for example. She noticed that her
neighbor, Mrs. Jenkins, always seemed lonely. One
day, Emma brought her a bouquet of flowers from her
backyard and stayed to chat for a while. Mrs. Jenkins'
eyes lit up, and she told Emma it was the nicest thing
anyone had done for her in a long time. That one act
of kindness made both Emma and Mrs. Jenkins feel
happier.

Another way to practice kindness is by helping
people who might feel left out. Imagine you're in the
cafeteria, and you see someone sitting by themselves.
Walking over and saying, "Can I sit with you?" can
make a huge difference. It's a simple way to show

someone they're not alone and that you care about including them.

Sometimes, showing kindness means standing up for others. Imagine a friend being teased for something they can't change, like the way they look or the clothes they wear. Speaking up and saying, "That's not cool—everyone deserves to be treated with respect," can help stop the teasing and show your friend that they're not alone.

Practicing kindness doesn't always mean doing something big. It can be as simple as smiling at someone, saying "thank you," or asking how their day is going. Imagine you're walking into your school building, and the crossing guard waves to you. Waving back and saying "Good morning!" is a small gesture, but it could brighten their day.

Empathy can also help you understand what someone else might need, even if they don't say it out loud. Think about your sibling having a rough day—they come home grumpy and slam the door to their room. Instead of getting annoyed, you might think about what could be bothering them. Maybe they had a tough day at school or got in trouble for something. You could knock on their door and say, "I noticed you're upset—do you want to talk about it?" Even if they don't want to talk, knowing you care could make them feel a little better.

Kindness and empathy can also extend to people you don't know. Imagine helping a stranger pick up something they dropped or donating your allowance to a cause you care about. These actions remind people that kindness exists, even from unexpected places.

Jake, for instance, saw a man drop his wallet while walking his dog in the park. Instead of ignoring it, Jake picked it up and ran after the man to return it. The man was so grateful and told Jake, "You've restored my faith in people." That small moment left a big impression on both of them.

Even when you're in a rush or having a bad day yourself, practicing kindness can make you feel better. Imagine being stressed about a test and feeling like nothing's going right. Then you hold the door open for someone, and they smile and say, "Thank you!" That tiny moment of connection can remind you that even in tough times, we all have the power to make each other's days a little brighter.

Kindness and empathy also matter when it comes to animals and the environment. Imagine leaving out a bowl of water for birds on a hot day, or picking up trash in your neighborhood to help keep it clean.

These acts show respect and care for the world around you, which is just as important as helping people.

Olivia started a kindness challenge with her friends at school. Each week, they tried to do one act of kindness for someone else, whether it was helping a younger student, writing a positive note, or cleaning up their school's playground. By the end of the month, they noticed that the whole school felt friendlier and more connected.

Fun activity: Create a "Helper's Journal"

Think about a special place where you can write down all the good things you've done to help others. It could be a notebook, a diary, or even a folder full of colorful pages. This would be your "Helper's Journal," a collection of all the ways you've made the world a little better. It's like creating your own story of kindness and empathy, and it's something you can look back on whenever you need a reminder of how powerful your actions can be.

To start your Helper's Journal, grab any notebook or even make your own by folding paper and stapling it together. The outside is your chance to get creative —decorate the cover with your favorite colors, stickers, or drawings that make you happy. You could even write something inspiring on the front, like "My Kind-ness Adventures" or "Acts of Awesomeness." It's your journal, so make it yours.

Inside, you can set up different sections to track the ways you've helped others. One section could be for small acts of kindness, like holding the door for someone or sharing your lunch. Another section could be for bigger projects, like volunteering with your family or starting a collection drive. You could even add a section for ideas—things you'd like to do in the future to help others.

Think about Elena, who started her Helper's Journal after noticing how much she enjoyed helping her classmates. One of her first entries was about tutoring her friend Max in math. She wrote, "Max was struggling with long division, and I explained it in a way that finally clicked for him. He said, 'You're a really good teacher,' and it made me feel proud!" Writing it down helped Elena remember how good it felt to help, and it motivated her to look for more ways to make a difference.

Each time you do something kind or helpful, take a moment to write about it in your journal. You don't need to write a long story—just a few sentences about what you did, how it made you feel, and how it affected the person you helped. For example, if you helped your neighbor rake leaves, you might write, "Today I helped Mr. Johnson rake his yard. He looked so happy and said it was the nicest surprise he'd had all week. I felt really strong using the big rake!"

Over time, your journal will fill up with all the ways you've spread kindness. Imagine flipping through the pages and seeing a list of all the times you've made someone smile or helped them through a tough day. It's like building a collection of happy memories, one act of kindness at a time.

You can also add pictures or drawings to your journal to make it even more special. Maybe you draw a picture of the playground you cleaned up or tape in a thank-you note you received. These little touches make your journal unique and remind you of the difference you've made.

For kids who love challenges, you can set kindness goals for yourself and track them in your journal. Maybe you decide to do one kind thing each day for a week or help three different people in one month. Write down your goals and check them off as you accomplish them. Imagine how satisfying it would feel to write, "Goal complete!" next to each one.

Marcus decided to set a goal to help five people in one month. He tracked each act in his journal, from helping his sister with her homework to baking cookies for his neighbor. By the end of the month, he had helped not just five people, but seven! He wrote at the bottom of the page, "I'm going to aim for ten next month!" His journal became a way to celebrate his efforts and challenge himself to keep going.

You can also use your Helper's Journal to reflect on what you've learned from helping others. Maybe you write about how it felt to help someone who was sad or how you came up with a creative solution to a problem. These reflections help you understand the impact of your actions and remind you that even small efforts can make a big difference.

Jenna wrote in her journal about a time she helped her younger brother build a birdhouse for a school project. "He was so frustrated when the pieces wouldn't fit together, but I helped him stay calm and figure it out. Seeing his face light up when we finished was the best feeling. I learned that patience can make a big difference." Writing it down helped Jenna see how much she'd grown by helping others.

Your journal can also be a place to write about the people who've helped you. Maybe you want to thank a friend who cheered you up or a teacher who explained something in a way that made sense. Writing about these moments reminds you that kindness goes both ways—it's something we give and receive.

Sam wrote about his coach in his Helper's Journal. "Coach Taylor stayed after practice to help me improve my free throws. He didn't have to, but he wanted to see me get better. I want to be like him and help others because it really makes a difference." By writing about his coach, Sam realized how much kindness inspires more kindness.

Once your journal starts to fill up, you might want to share it with others. Maybe you show it to your family or a teacher, or you use it to inspire your friends to start their own journals. Imagine a whole group of kids creating Helper's Journals and sharing their stories of kindness. Together, you'd be spreading even more positivity and making your community a better place.

8

SOCIAL WORK AROUND THE WORLD

Let's start in Kenya, a country in East Africa. In some areas, social workers spend a lot of time helping children who've lost their parents to illness or other hardships. Imagine a social worker named Amina visiting a small village. She meets a group of kids living with their grandmother, who struggles to provide for them. Amina helps the family find support, like food programs and school supplies. She also connects them with counselors who help the kids cope with losing their parents.

One unique thing about social work in Kenya is the focus on community. People often come together to help each other, and social workers work closely with villages and extended families to solve problems.

It's not just about helping individuals—it's about strengthening the whole community.

Now imagine traveling to Japan, where social work often focuses on elderly people. Japan has one of the oldest populations in the world, and many older adults need help with things like health care, transportation, or even just having someone to talk to.

A social worker named Hiroshi might visit an elderly woman named Yumi, who lives alone and struggles to get to her doctor's appointments. Hiroshi helps arrange a transportation service and makes regular visits to check on her. During one visit, Yumi tells him, "I feel less lonely knowing you'll stop by."

In Japan, respecting elders is a big part of the culture, and social workers help honor that tradition by ensuring older adults are cared for and valued.

Let's head to Brazil, where social workers often focus on children and families in crowded cities called favelas. These neighborhoods can be vibrant and full of life, but they also face challenges like poverty and lack of resources.

Imagine a social worker named Camila running a program for kids in a favela. She helps them with schoolwork, organizes soccer games, and teaches them about staying safe. Camila also works with parents, helping them find jobs or access health care. For her, social work isn't just about solving problems—it's about creating opportunities for families to thrive.

Now picture a snowy village in Norway. Social workers here often focus on helping people with mental health challenges. In Norway, there's a strong belief that everyone deserves support, no matter what they're going through.

A social worker named Erik might visit a teenager named Lars, who's been feeling anxious and doesn't want to go to school. Erik talks with Lars and his parents, helping them understand what's happening and finding ways to make school feel less scary. He also connects Lars with a counselor who helps him build confidence.

In Norway, social workers often work as part of a team, including doctors, teachers, and other professionals. They believe in working together to support the whole person, not just one part of their life.

In India, social work can look very different depending on whether it's in a big city or a small village. Imagine a social worker named Priya working in a rural area. She meets a group of women who want to start their own businesses, like weaving baskets or raising chickens. Priya helps them learn about loans and savings, giving them the tools to create a better future for their families.

In India, social workers often focus on empowering people to solve their own problems. They don't just give people help—they teach them how to help themselves, which can lead to lasting change.

Let's journey to the United States, where social workers tackle a wide range of challenges. In one city, a social worker named Alex might spend the morning helping a homeless family find shelter and the afternoon visiting a school to talk to kids about bullying.

In the U.S., social work is all about flexibility. Social workers are everywhere—in hospitals, schools, neighborhoods, and even online. They wear many hats, adapting to the needs of the people they're helping.

Finally, imagine Australia, where social workers often focus on supporting Indigenous communities. A social worker named Mia might visit a remote area to help families gain access to clean water or education. Mia listens carefully to the community's needs, making sure the solutions respect their culture and traditions.

Global efforts to support vulnerable groups

Around the world, social workers are part of teams that respond to emergencies like hurricanes, earthquakes, and wildfires. They aren't just handing out supplies—they're also listening to people's stories, helping them find safety, and offering comfort during a scary time.

One example is Maria, a social worker in the Philippines, where typhoons often hit hard. After a massive storm destroyed homes in a coastal town, Maria worked with a team to set up a shelter for families who had nowhere to go. She organized activities for kids, like drawing and games, to help them feel safe and cared for while their parents figured out their next steps.

Maria also listened to people who had lost everything. She reminded them that they weren't alone and connected them to programs that helped them rebuild their homes. When one family moved into a new house built with the community's help, they told Maria, "You gave us hope when we thought we had none."

In many parts of the world, social workers also help refugees—people who've had to leave their homes because of war, violence, or natural disasters. Imagine having to pack up your life and move to a new country where you don't know the language or customs. Refugees face challenges like finding housing, getting jobs, and adjusting to a new culture.

In Germany, a social worker named Klaus met a family who had fled their home in Syria. The family was scared and didn't know how to navigate life in a new country. Klaus helped them find an apartment, enroll the kids in school, and learn the basics of the German language.

One day, the youngest child, Lina, ran up to Klaus with a big smile. She said, "I made a new friend at school today!" That moment reminded Klaus why his work mattered—he wasn't just helping the family survive; he was helping them build a new life.

Refugee camps are another place where social workers play a big role. Imagine a camp filled with tents, where thousands of people are waiting for a safe place to call home. Social workers in these camps do everything from organizing food distribution to offering counseling for people who've been through traumatic experiences.

One social worker, Amina, worked in a camp in Uganda. She helped reunite children who had been separated from their families during their journey. Amina also created a "safe space" for kids, where they could play, learn, and feel cared for. Seeing the kids laugh and play brought light to a place that could feel dark and overwhelming.

Disaster relief and refugee support aren't the only

global efforts social workers are involved in. They also help people affected by poverty, disease, and other challenges that make life difficult. In South Africa, for example, social workers often work with families affected by HIV/AIDS. They provide education about the disease, help people get medical care, and offer emotional support to those who feel scared or isolated.

In one town, a social worker named Sipho met a woman named Thandi, who had just found out she was HIV-positive. Thandi felt ashamed and didn't want to tell anyone, not even her family. Sipho listened without judgment and helped Thandi understand that having HIV didn't mean her life was over. Over time, Thandi found the courage to share her story with her family, and Sipho connected her with a support group where she met others going through the same thing.

In another part of the world, like Haiti, social workers focus on rebuilding communities after earthquakes. A social worker named Jean helped a small town recover after an earthquake destroyed many homes and schools. Jean worked with local leaders to rebuild a school, and when it opened, he was there to see the kids walk into their new classrooms.

Global efforts to support vulnerable groups often

involve working with teams from different countries. Social workers might partner with doctors, teachers, and other helpers to make sure people get what they need. Imagine a team arriving in a flooded area with supplies like food, medicine, and clean water. Social workers on the team make sure the supplies go to the people who need them most, especially kids, elderly people, and those with disabilities.

One inspiring example comes from a group of social workers who traveled to Nepal after a massive earthquake. They worked with local communities to create safe spaces for kids who had lost their homes. These spaces became places where kids could learn, play, and feel cared for while their families worked on rebuilding.

Social workers also help during pandemics, like when COVID-19 spread around the world. In countries like Italy and India, social workers delivered food and medicine to families stuck in their homes. They also checked in on elderly people living alone, making sure they had everything they needed.

One social worker, Priya, rode her bike through the streets of her city in India, delivering meals to families who couldn't leave their homes. She said, "I couldn't stay still knowing people needed help." Her efforts inspired others in her community to join in, showing how kindness and determination can spread.

Cultural sensitivity and diversity

Cultural sensitivity is about understanding and respecting other people's beliefs, traditions, and ways of doing things, even if they're different from your own. It's an important skill for social workers because they help people from all kinds of backgrounds. Imagine working with a family who speaks a different language or has traditions you've never heard of. Being open-minded and curious helps social workers build trust and connect with the people they're helping.

Let's take an example. Imagine a social worker named Javier in Mexico who helps families living in rural areas. One day, he visits a family celebrating Día de los Muertos, or Day of the Dead. The family has built an altar with flowers, photos, and food to honor their ancestors. At first, Javier doesn't know much about the tradition, but he listens as the family explains its meaning. By showing respect and interest, Javier builds a strong relationship with the family, making it easier to work together.

Social workers also have to be mindful of how

people communicate differently. In some cultures, it's polite to look someone in the eye when you're talking to them, while in others, it's more respectful to avoid eye contact. Imagine being a social worker in Japan, where bowing is a common way to greet someone. A social worker who bows instead of shaking hands shows they understand and respect the culture.

Think about a social worker named Priya in India who helps women start small businesses. One of the women, Asha, is hesitant to speak up in meetings because in her community, it's considered polite to let others talk first. Priya notices this and gently encourages Asha to share her ideas. By understanding Asha's culture and supporting her in a way that feels comfortable, Priya helps her gain confidence.

Cultural sensitivity isn't just about traditions—it's also about understanding people's challenges. Imagine a refugee family moving to a new country where everything feels different. They might not understand the language, the weather, or even how to use public transportation. A social worker who takes the time to learn about the family's culture can help them feel more at home.

In Canada, a social worker named Thomas works with Indigenous communities. He knows that many of the families he helps have faced unfair treatment in the past, so he takes extra care to listen and learn about their traditions. When a family invites him to a powwow—a special gathering with dancing, music, and ceremonies—Thomas feels honored. By participating respectfully, he shows he values their culture and wants to support them in a way that feels right to them.

Sometimes, cultural sensitivity means understanding that people have different ways of solving problems. Imagine a social worker named Elena in Italy helping a family who's having a conflict. Instead of just talking to one person, she brings the whole extended family together because in their culture, big decisions are often made as a group. By adapting to their way of doing things, Elena helps the family work through their challenges more effectively.

Social workers also use cultural sensitivity when helping kids. Imagine a child named Samira who moves to a new school in England and feels left out because her classmates don't understand her traditions. A school social worker might encourage Samira to share about her culture during a class presentation. This not only helps Samira feel proud of her background but also teaches her classmates about diversity.

Diversity is what makes the world so interesting.

It's like a giant puzzle where each piece is unique but fits together to create a beautiful picture. Social workers celebrate diversity by treating every person they meet with kindness and respect, no matter where they come from or what they believe.

Cultural sensitivity also means being careful not to make assumptions. Imagine meeting someone who wears traditional clothing or speaks with an accent. Instead of guessing what their life is like, you could ask questions and listen to their story. Social workers know that everyone's experience is different, and the best way to understand is to be curious and respectful.

9

THE FUTURE OF SOCIAL WORK

One big change is the use of telehealth services. Telehealth means using video calls or phone calls to connect with people who need help. Imagine a family living in a small town where there aren't many social workers nearby. Instead of having to drive hours to meet someone in person, they can talk to a social worker from their own home using a computer or smartphone.

A social worker named Jenna works in a city but helps people in rural areas through telehealth. One of her clients is Mateo, a teenager who feels anxious about going to school. Jenna meets with Mateo and his parents over video calls to talk about his feelings and come up with strategies to help him feel more confident. Even though they're miles apart, Jenna's support makes a big difference for Mateo.

Another way technology is helping social work is through apps. Imagine an app that helps people find the resources they need, like food banks, shelters, or counseling services. Instead of spending hours searching for help, people can open the app, type in what they're looking for, and get a list of nearby options.

One popular app is called Aunt Bertha, which helps people in the U.S. find services in their community. A social worker named Raj uses the app to help his clients. When a single mom named Clara needs help paying her utility bills, Raj types her zip code into the app and finds a program that offers financial assistance. Clara says, "I didn't even know this program existed!" The app helps Raj connect Clara to the resources she needs, faster and easier than ever before.

Some social workers are even using virtual reality (VR) to help people. VR creates a computer-generated world that feels real when you wear special goggles. Imagine a social worker helping someone who's scared of public speaking by using VR to practice talking in front of a virtual audience.

A social worker named Emily works with kids

who've been through difficult experiences. She uses VR to create calming, virtual environments, like a peaceful beach or a quiet forest, where kids can relax and feel safe. One of Emily's clients, a boy named Liam, says, "It feels like I'm really there, and it helps me forget about my worries for a little while."

Technology is also helping social workers stay organized. Imagine a busy social worker juggling meetings, phone calls, and paperwork. New tools like online databases and scheduling apps make it easier for them to keep track of everything.

Thomas, a social worker in Canada, uses an app that lets him store important information about his clients in one secure place. Instead of flipping through stacks of papers, he can quickly pull up a file on his tablet during a meeting. "It saves me so much time," Thomas says, "and I can spend more of that time actually helping people."

Social media is another tool social workers are using to reach people. Imagine a social worker creating a video about how to handle stress and sharing it on platforms like Instagram or TikTok. People who watch the video can learn new skills and feel supported, even if they've never met the social worker in person.

In Australia, a social worker named Mia runs a

popular social media account where she posts tips on mental health and shares stories of people overcoming challenges. Her posts inspire thousands of followers, including a teenager named Zoe, who says, "Mia's videos helped me realize it's okay to ask for help."

Technology is also making it easier for social workers to work together. Imagine social workers in different countries sharing ideas and learning from each other through online forums or video conferences. They can discuss what's working in their communities and come up with new ways to help people.

A social worker named Ahmed in Egypt recently joined an online workshop with social workers from around the world. He learned about a successful program in Brazil that helps kids stay in school and shared the idea with his team back home. Ahmed says, "It's amazing how technology lets us connect and share solutions, no matter where we are."

Of course, technology isn't perfect, and there are challenges to using it. Some people don't have access to the internet or devices like smartphones, which can make it harder for them to use telehealth or apps. Social workers are working to solve these problems by finding creative ways to reach people who might be left out.

For example, in a rural village in India, a social worker named Priya organizes "digital days" where families can come to a community center and use tablets to connect with services. Priya helps them navigate the technology and ensures they get the support they need.

Another challenge is making sure people's information stays private. Social workers use secure platforms and follow strict rules to protect the people they help. It's like having a locked diary where only the social worker and their client have the key.

10

ARE YOU READY TO BE A SOCIAL WORKER?

Being a great social worker starts with kindness. Kindness is like a bridge—it helps you connect with people, no matter where they come from or what they're going through. Think about the times you've helped a friend, shared something with a sibling, or done something nice for someone just because it felt right. That's the kind of kindness social workers show every day.

Then there's empathy, which is like putting on someone else's shoes and walking a mile in them. It's about imagining how someone else feels and trying to understand their perspective. Maybe you've seen a classmate looking sad and thought, "What would make me feel better if I were in their place?" That thought is empathy, and it's a superpower that helps social workers connect with people on a deeper level.

Let's not forget about listening—really listening. Great social workers don't just hear words; they pay attention to feelings, body language, and what's not being said. Imagine sitting with someone who's upset and letting them share their story without interrupting or judging. Sometimes, just knowing someone is truly listening can make all the difference.

Problem-solving is another key part of being a social worker. It's like being a detective, figuring out what's wrong and coming up with creative solutions. Maybe you've helped a friend who couldn't figure out a tricky math problem or worked with your family to plan a fun day everyone could enjoy. Those moments of thinking and teamwork are great practice for the kind of problem-solving social workers do.

Determination is what keeps social workers going, even when things get tough. Imagine trying to put together a puzzle with a missing piece. It might feel frustrating, but you keep searching because you know the picture won't be complete until you find it. Social workers face challenges like this all the time, and their determination helps them find solutions, no matter how long it takes.

Being patient is also important. Change doesn't

happen overnight, and people don't always open up right away. Great social workers understand that building trust takes time. Think about the times you've waited for something exciting, like a birthday or a trip. That same kind of patience helps social workers stay calm and focused as they support people through their journeys.

Communication is another big part of the job. Social workers need to explain ideas clearly and help people feel comfortable sharing their thoughts. Imagine being on a team where everyone works together toward a goal. Great communication helps the team stay connected and strong, just like it helps social workers build strong relationships with the people they help.

Let's not forget the importance of learning. Great social workers are always curious and eager to know more. They learn about different cultures, new ways to solve problems, and the latest tools and technology. Imagine your favorite subject at school. The more you learn about it, the better you understand it—and the more confident you feel. That same excitement for learning helps social workers stay sharp and ready to help in the best ways possible.

Social workers also need a strong sense of fairness. They believe everyone deserves respect, no matter who they are or what they've been through. Imagine playing a game where everyone gets a chance to win, not just the fastest or strongest players. Social workers work to create fairness in real life, making sure everyone has the support they need to succeed.

Courage is another important trait. Helping people isn't always easy. Sometimes it means standing up for what's right, even when it feels scary. Maybe you've spoken up for a friend who was being treated unfairly or tried something new even though you were nervous. Those moments of bravery are what make social workers strong.

Finally, great social workers have big hearts. They care deeply about making the world a better place and aren't afraid to work hard to make it happen. Imagine planting a garden, knowing it will take time and effort to grow. Social workers plant seeds of kindness, support, and change, trusting that their efforts will make a difference, even if they don't see the results right away.

Being a great social worker doesn't mean you have to do it all at once. It starts with small actions, like helping a friend, standing up for someone, or taking time to listen. Every time you practice kindness, empathy, and problem-solving, you're building the skills that make a difference.

Picture yourself as a social worker one day. Who would you help? What challenges would you tackle? Maybe you'd work with kids, families, or even entire communities. Or maybe you'd focus on protecting animals, helping the environment, or supporting people during tough times. Whatever path you choose, you'll be using your unique strengths to make the world a better place.

The future of social work is bright, and it's waiting for people like you—people who care, who listen, and who believe in the power of helping others. Whether you're ready to take the first step today or dreaming of making a big impact someday, you already have what it takes to make a difference.

Picture yourself as a social worker in the future. What does your day look like? Are you meeting with families to solve problems, running programs in your community, or working with animals? Are you helping people face-to-face or using technology to reach them? Your answers can help you imagine the kind of impact you want to make.

It's okay if you don't know exactly what kind of social work interests you yet. These questions aren't about figuring everything out—they're about starting to think about the possibilities. Every time you help someone, you're practicing the skills that social workers use every day. And as you grow, you'll find even more ways to make a difference.

Helping others isn't just about the actions you take —it's also about the kind of person you are. Are you someone who listens? Someone who notices when others need help? Someone who believes in fairness and kindness? These are all qualities that make a great social worker.

Now imagine the world as a giant jigsaw puzzle. Each piece represents a person, a community, or a need. Social workers are like puzzle solvers—they bring the pieces together, helping people and communities fit into a bigger, brighter picture. And you could be one of those puzzle solvers.

Think about the questions again: How do you help others? What kind of social work interests you? These aren't just questions—they're the start of your journey toward making the world a better place. And the best part is, you're already on your way. Every time you listen, care, and take action, you're practicing the heart of what it means to be a social worker.

APPENDIX

Movies That Inspire

1. Akeelah and the Bee

Akeelah is a girl from South Los Angeles who enters a national spelling bee. Along the way, she inspires her community and learns that asking for help can lead to amazing things. This movie shows the power of determination and teamwork.

2. The Blind Side

Based on a true story, this film follows Michael Oher, a teenager without a stable home, and the family that takes him in and helps him achieve his dreams. It's a moving story about the importance of seeing potential in others and offering support.

3. Inside Out

While it's an animated movie about emotions, it offers a wonderful lesson in understanding feelings—both your own and others'. Social workers often help people navigate emotions, making this movie a great way to think about empathy and care.

4. Dolphin Tale

This film is based on the true story of Winter, a dolphin with a prosthetic tail. It's about compassion, teamwork, and how people can come together to help those in need—whether they're human or animal.

5. Wonder Woman (2017)

While it's a superhero movie, Wonder Woman's mission to protect and help others fits right into the idea of making the world better. It's a reminder that courage and a desire to do good can make you a hero in your own way.

Websites to Explore

1. UNICEF (www.unicef.org)

This website shares stories about kids around the world and how organizations like UNICEF help them with education, clean water, and health care. It's a great way to see how people are working together to solve global problems.

2. DoSomething.org

Focused on young people, this website offers tons of ideas for projects you can do to help your community. From organizing drives to advocating for causes you care about, it's full of ways to get involved.

3. World Wildlife Fund (www.worldwildlife.org)

If you're interested in helping animals and protecting the planet, this site is a great place to start. You can learn about endangered species and ways to support conservation efforts.

4. Sesame Workshop (www.sesameworkshop.org)

The creators of Sesame Street offer resources for kids and families about kindness, emotional health, and helping others. It's a fun and interactive way to learn more about being a good friend and community member.

5. National Geographic Kids (kids.nationalgeographic.com)

Explore stories about kids making a difference, animals being rescued, and the planet being protected. This site inspires action by showing how others are already making an impact.

www.ingramcontent.com/pod-product-compliance
Ingram Content Group UK Ltd.
Pitfield, Milton Keynes, MK11 3LW, UK
UKHW030725020125
452872UK00006B/42